"Frankly, My Dear..."

Gone with the Wind Memorabilia

Margaret Mitchell Memento Mori

Engraved invitation to the funeral of Mrs. John R. Marsh (Margaret Mitchell) at Spring Hill Mortuary, Atlanta.

Margaret Mitchell Memorial Issue of the *Atlanta Journal Magazine*, 18 Dec. 1949. The color portrait on the cover was photographed in 1947. [40 pp., 11x15]

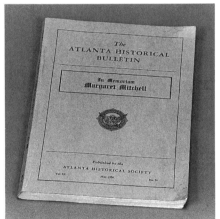

"In Memoriam: Margaret Mitchell," the *Atlanta Historical Bulletin* (May 1950), 150 pp., paperbound, illustrated.

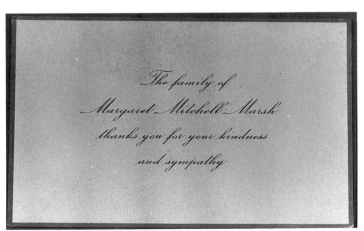

An engraved acknowledgment of sympathy from the family of Margaret Mitchell Marsh.

When a Japanese publisher openly pirated *Gone with the Wind* in the late 1930s, the publisher gave Margaret Mitchell a porcelain doll in lieu of compensation. Mitchell named the doll by the publisher's remark that accompanied the doll—"O-so-solly." Mitchell is shown here with the doll at the Atlanta Red Cross headquarters. She offered the doll for auction to raise funds for the Red Cross during World War II. (Early 1940s.)

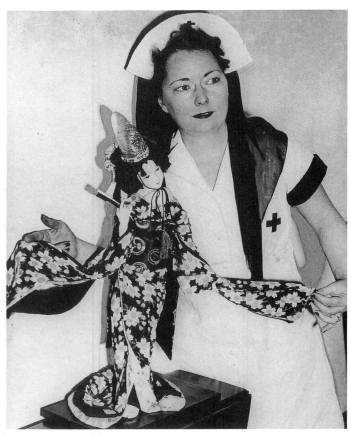

A full-color photograph of Margaret Mitchell—made in her living room at 1268 Piedmont Avenue NE, Atlanta, in November 1947—appeared in the Margaret Mitchell Memorial Issue of the *Atlanta Journal Magazine* (18 December 1949).

Gone with the Wind: The Book

Margaret Mitchell's *Gone with the Wind* was published by the Macmillan Publishing Company of New York City on 30 June 1936. At 1,037 pages, Mitchell's epic tale of the Civil War South weighed almost three pounds. The book was printed by the Ferris Printing Company and bound in gray buckram. The dust jacket was designed by George Carlson. The retail price of the book was $3.00.

Gone with the Wind was originally scheduled to appear in May 1936, but a lucrative contractual agreement with the Book-of-the-Month Club delayed publication until the last day of June. When that agreement was executed the presses were already rolling, producing copies showing May as the publication date. Therefore, a true "first edition" of *Gone with the Wind* will read, on the verso of the title page, "Set-up and electrotyped. Published May, 1936."

After the agreement with the Book-of-the-Month Club, the publisher simply changed the copyright date to "June, 1936"; no official notice was ever taken of the copies produced with the May date. Some collectors state that fewer than 5,000 copies were printed with "May, 1936" on the copyright page, although no specific proof has been produced to substantiate this assertion.

The First Edition

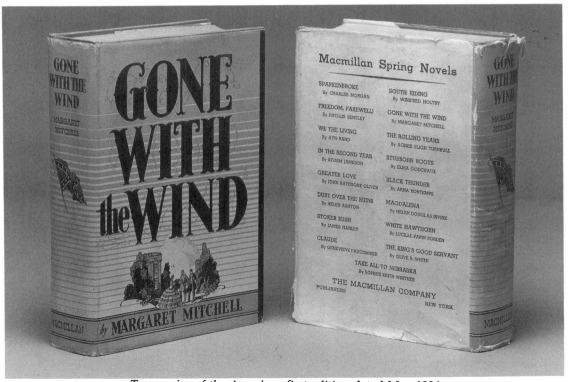

Two copies of the American first edition dated May 1936,
showing the front and back of the original dust jacket.

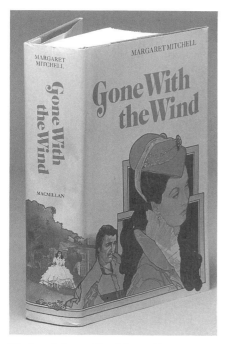

Undated. Issued by Macmillan with no date; purchased in 1978; 733 pp., hardbound with dust jacket.

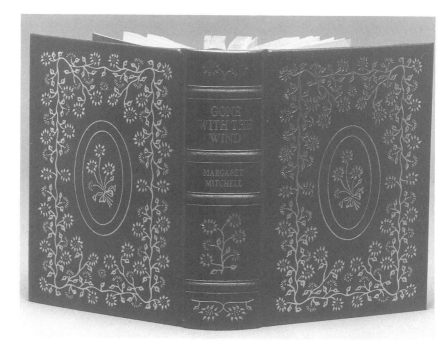

1984. An edition issued by the Southern Classics Library of Birmingham, Alabama; 1,037 pp., leatherbound.

American Paperbound Editions

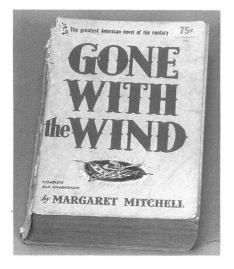

1954. The first pocketbook paperbound edition of *Gone with the Wind* published by Permabooks in March 1954; 862 pp.,, $.75.

1961. Macmillan paperbacks edition; 1,037 pp., $2.85.

A black and white poster advertising the 1967 Pocket Books paperbound edition.

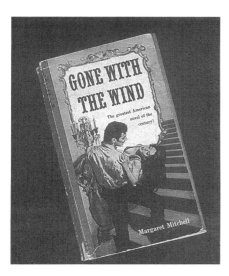

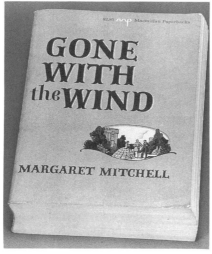

1960. Permabooks, paperbound edition; 862 pp., $0.75.

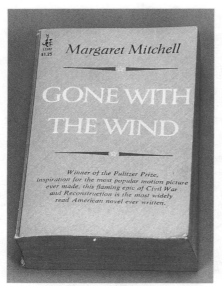

1967. Pocket Books edition;
862 pp., $1.25.

1969. Pocket Books edition;
862 pp., $1.25.

1972. Flare Books edition, published
by Avon Books; 1,037 pp., $3.95.

Foreign Editions of Gone with the Wind

Argentina. *Lo que el vieno se llevo* (Buenos Aires. Editorial
Americana, 1954) 995 pp., paperbound; a pirated edition
produced without the permission of Macmillan,
the original publisher in the United States.

Austria. *Vom Winde verweht* (Wien:
Verlag Buch und Welt, 1974)
925 pp., hardbound
with dust jacket.

Austria. *Vom Winde verweht* (Wien: Buchgemeinschaft, [1965?])
896 pp., hardbound with dust jacket; a book club edition
produced under license from German publishers.

Belgium. *Autant en
emporte le vent* (Bruges:
Editions Brugeoieses,
1947) 828 pp., paper-
bound; this edition was
produced with special
permission from the
French publisher
because of an acute
shortage of paper
in France.

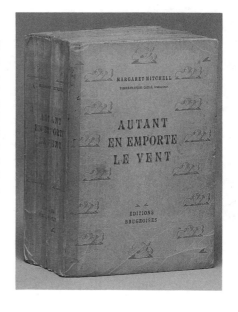

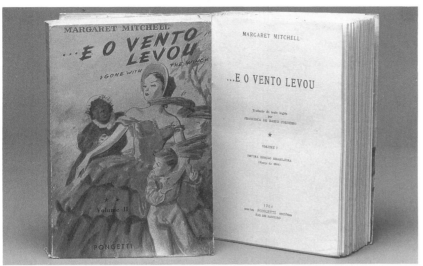

Brazil. *E O Vento Levou* (Rio de Janeiro: Iramãos Pongetti Editöres, 1940)
805 pp., 2 vols., paperbound.

Bulgaria. [*Gone with the Wind*]
(Sofia, 1990), 1,226 pp., 2 vols.,
casebound, no jackets.

Brazil. *E O vento Levou* (São Paulo:
Hemus-Livaria Editora, 1973)
801 pp., paperbound.

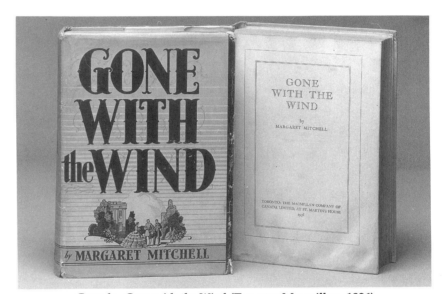

Canada. *Gone with the Wind* (Toronto: Macmillan, 1936)
1,037 pp., casebound with dust jacket.

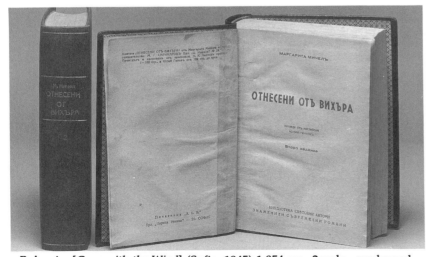

Bulgaria. [*Gone with the Wind*] (Sofia, 1945) 1,054 pp., 2 vols., casebound.

Canada. *Gone with the Wind* (Toronto: Macmillan,
1939) 391 pp., paperbound; motion picture edition,
illustrated with color photographs from the film.

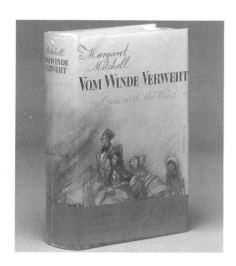

Germany. *Vom Winde verweht*
(Hamburg: Claassen Verlag)
1,008 pp., casebound with dust jacket.
This current German edition shares
the basic dust jacket design
of the first edition of 1937.

Germany. *Vom Winde verweht* (Berlin: Deutsche Buch Gemeinschaft,
1938) 1,008 pp., 2 vols., casebound; a deluxe book club edition.

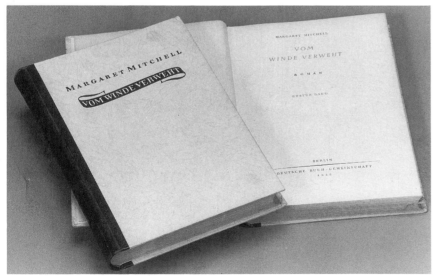

Germany. *Vom Winde verweht* (Berlin: Deutsche Buch Gemeinschaft,
1948) 934 pp., 2 vols., casebound; also a deluxe book club edition.

Germany. The first installment of a serialization of *Vom Winde verweht* in the newspaper *Neue Post*, printed in Dusseldorf, 21 February 1959.

Germany. *Gone with the Wind* (Berlin: Velhagen und Klasing, 1967) 67 pp., casebound. This collection of selected passages is accompanied by a 56-page paper-bound booklet of "Annotations" defining English terms in German. The set was intended for use in English classes in Germany.

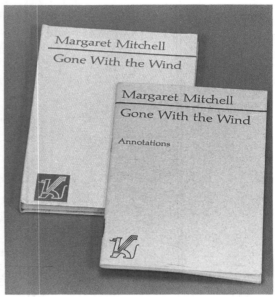

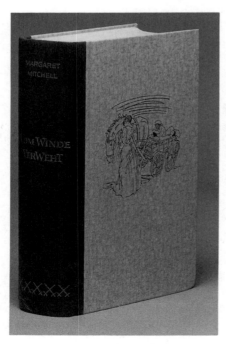

Germany. *Vom Winde verweht* (Stuttgart, 1964) 916 pp., casebound, with an illustration stamped on the front cover; a book club edition.

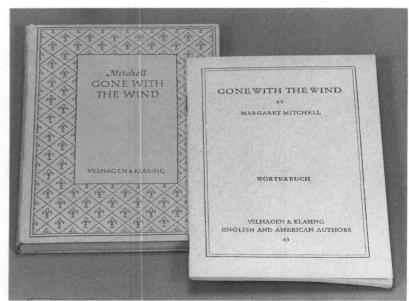

Germany. An undated earlier edition of English excerpts from *GWTW* with the German "Annotations," published before 1967.

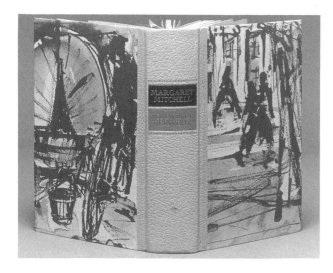

Germany. *Vom Winde verweht* (Stuttgart: Fackelverlag, 1968)
916 pp., casebound, with illustrations on the front and back covers;
a book club edition.

[left] Germany. *Vom Winde verweht*
(Hamburg: RORORO Taschenbuch
Ausgabe, 1968) 918 pp., paperbound;
a book club edition.

[right] Germany. *Vom Winde verweht*
(Frankfurt am Main, 1971) 947 pp.,
casebound with dust jacket;
a book club edition.

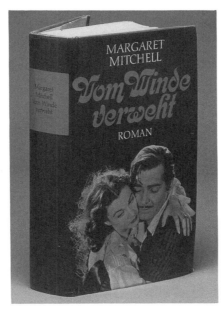

[left] Germany. *Vom Winde verweht* (Struttgart, 1970)
947 pp., casebound with dust jacket;
a book club edition.

[right] Germany. *Vom Winde verweht* (Gutersloh,
1979) 925 pp., casebound with dust jacket;
a Bertelsmann Book Club edition.

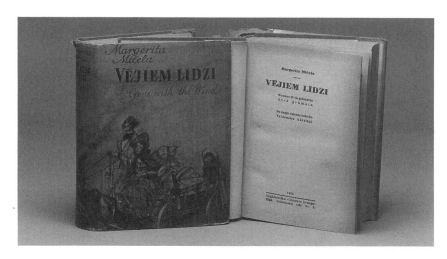

Latvia. *Vejiem Lidzi* (Riga, 1938)
1,158 pp., 2 vols., casebound with dust jackets.

Latvia. *Vejiem Lidzi* (n.p.: Gramatu Draugs, 1950) 726 pp., 3 vols., paperbound.

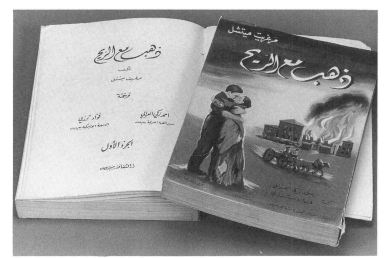

Lebanon. [*Gone with the Wind*] (Beirut: Dar Assakafa, 1958)
2 vols., paperbound.

Mexico. *Lo que el viento se llevo* (Mexico City, 1953) 1,106 pp., casebound with dust jacket; a pirated edition.

The Netherlands. *Gejaagd door de Wind* (The Hague: M. C. Stok, [1937?]) 1,001 pp., 3 vols.; casebound with dust jackets; illustrated in color and black and white by Anton Pieck.

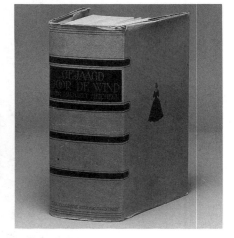

The Netherlands. *Gejaagd door de Wind* (The Hague: M. C. Stok, [1950?] 1,001 pp., casebound with dust jacket; illustrated in color and black and white by Anton Pieck; a deluxe edition of 3 vols. bound as one.

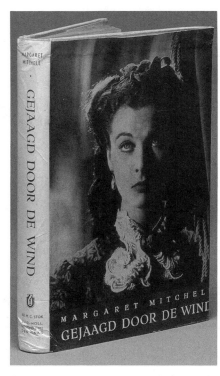

The Netherlands. *Gejaagd door de Wind* (The Hague: M. C. Stok, [1966?]) 632 pp., casebound with jackets; illustrated with photographs from the motion picture

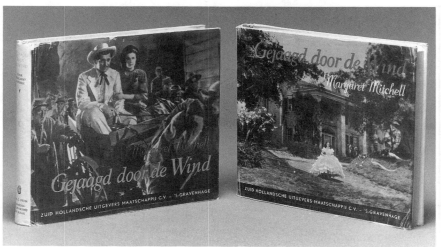

The Netherlands. *Gejaagd door de Wind* (The Hague: M. C. Stok, [1965?]) 801 pp., 2 vols., casebound with dust jackets; illustrated with photographs from the motion picture.

The Netherlands. *Gejaagd door de Wind* (The Hague: M. C. Stok, [1968?]) 743 pp., casebound with dust jacket.

Norway. *Tatt av vinden* (Oslo: H. Aschehoug, 1938) 1,283 pp., 3 vols., casebound with dust jackets.

The Netherlands. Two recent editions of *Gejaagd door de Wind*: [left] (The Hague: M.C. Stok, 1980) 743 pp., casebound with dust jacket, illustrated with photographs from the motion picture; [right] (The Hague: M. C. Stok, 1985) 743 pp., paperbound.

Norway. A 1937 leaflet advertising the 3-vol. edition of *Tatt av vinden* published by H. Aschehoug in Oslo.

Norway. A 1937 poster advertising *Tatt av vinden*.

Norway. A 1938 pamphlet advertising *Tatt av vinden*.

Norway. *Tatt av vinden* (Oslo: Aschehougs Fonteneboker, 1964) 1,074 pp., 2 vols., paperbound, in cardboard slipcase.

Norway. Poster from the 1970s advertising the edition of *Tatt av vinden* published by Aschehoug of Oslo. [11½ x 17½]

Norway. *Tatt av vinden* (Oslo: Aschehoug, 1984) 890 pp., casebound with dust jacket.

Poland. *Przeminelo z Wiatrem* (Warsaw: Wydawnictwo J. Przeworskiego, 1939) 1,478 pp., 2 vols., casebound with dust jackets.

Norway. *Tatt av vinden* (Oslo: Norske Bokklubber, 1971) 994 pp., 2 vols., casebound with dust jackets.

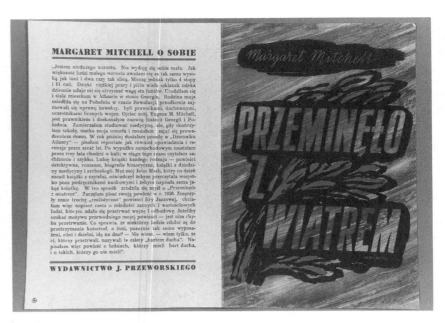

Poland. A four-page, four-color brochure advertising *Przeminelo z Wiatrem* in 1939; front and back covers are shown.

Poland. *Przeminelo z Wiatrem* (Warsaw: Mieczyslaw Fuksiewicz, 1949) 1,455 pp., 2 vols., paperbound.

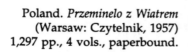

Poland. *Przeminelo z Wiatrem* (Warsaw: Czytelnik, 1957) 1,297 pp., 4 vols., paperbound.

Poland. *Przeminelo z Wiatrem* (Warsaw: Czytelnik, 1977) 1,141 pp., 3 vols., paperbound.

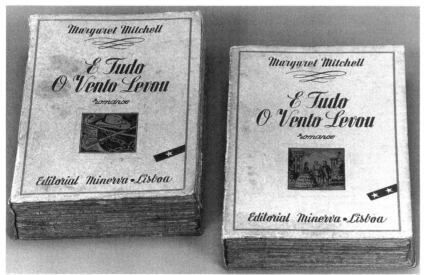

Portugal. *E Tudo O Vento Levou* (Lisbon: Editorial Minerva, 1954) 1,030 pp., 2 vols., paperbound.

Portugal. *E Tudo O Vento Levou* (Lisbon: Editorial Minerva, 1965) 1,170 pp., 2 vols., paperbound, with dust jackets.

Portugal. *E Tudo O Vento Levou*
(Lisbon: Circulo Leitores, 1980-1981)
903 pp., 2 vols., casebound with dust jackets;
a book club edition.

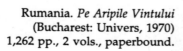

Rumania. *Pe Aripile Vantului* (Bucharest:
Editura Nationala GH. Mecu, 1943)
1,244 pp., 2 vols., paperbound.

Rumania. *Pe Aripile Vintului*
(Bucharest: Univers, 1970)
1,262 pp., 2 vols., paperbound.

Russia. [*Gone with the Wind*] (Moscow, 1990)
971 pp., casebound, no dust jackets; a pirated edition.

Sweden. *Borta med Vinden* (Stockholm: Medéns Forlags
Aktiebolag, 1937) 1,199 pp., 2 vols., casebound.

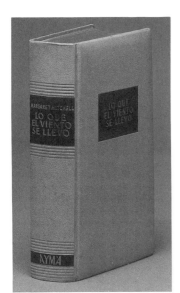

Spain. *Lo que el viento se llevo* (Barcelona:
Aymá, 1961) 918 pp., leatherbound;
illustrated with photographs from the motion picture.

Sweden. *Borta med Vinden* (Stockholm: Medéns, 1937)
1,199 pp., 2 vols., paperbound.

Spain. *Allo que el vent s'endugue* (Barcelona:
Aymá, S.A. Editora, 1977) 875 pp., paperbound.

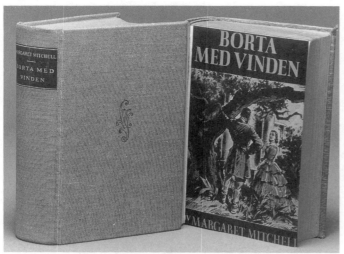

Sweden. *Borta med Vinden* (Stockholm: Medéns Forlags Aktiebolag, 1941) 1,199 pp., two paperbound volumes specially bound in one casebound edition.

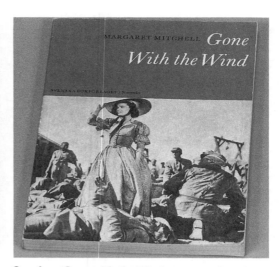

Sweden. *Gone with the Wind*, excerpted and edited by Arne Rudskoger (Stockholm: Svenska Bokforlaget, 1963) 201 pp., paperbound. Prepared as a text for English courses in Swedish schools.

Sweden. *Borta med Vinden* (Stockholm: Bonniers Folkbibliotek, 1953) 552 pp., casebound with dust jacket.

Sweden. *Borta med Vinden* (Stockholm: Albert Bonniers Forlag, 1970) 1,048 pp., 3 vols., casebound with dust jackets.

Sweden. *Borta med Vinden* (Stockholm: Bonniers Folkbibliotek, 1961) 552 pp., casebound, in cardboard slipcase.

Sweden. *Borta med Vinden* (Stockholm:
Albert Bonniers Forlag, 1982) 1,048 pp., 2 vols.,
casebound with dust jackets; printed in Hungary.

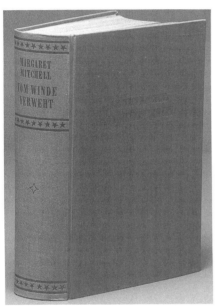

Switzerland. *Vom Winde verweht*
(Bern: Albert Scherz Verlag, 1948)
888 pp., casebound; issued under
license from the German publisher.

Taiwan. [*Gone with the Wind*]
(Taipei, [1960?]) 749 pp., casebound.

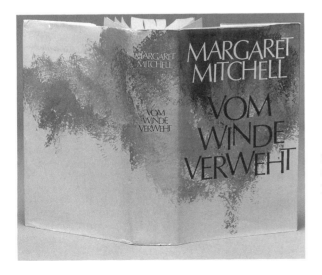

Switzerland. *Vom Winde verweht* (Bern: Neue Schweizer Bibliotek, 1971)
824 pp., casebound with dust jacket; a book club edition
produced under license from the German publisher.

Taiwan. [*Gone with the Wind*] (Taipei, [1960?])
749 pp., 2 vols., paperbound.

Thailand. [*Gone with the Wind*] (Bangkok, n.d.)
2,094 pp., 2 vols., paperbound.

Thailand. [*Gone with the Wind*]
(n.p., [1965?]) 7 vols., casebound;
a pirated edition in the
Thai language.

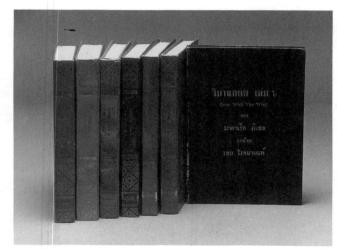

Taiwan. *Gone with the Wind* (n.p., 1965)
120 pp., paperbound.
A digest with Chinese translation
used as a text to teach English
in Taiwanese schools.

Turkey. *Rüzgar Gibi Geçti* (Istanbul: Hilmi Kitabevi, 1942-1944) 1,596 pp., 3 vols., paperbound. Vol. 1, published in 1942, has a German illustration on the cover; vol. 2 (1943) uses an Italian illustration on the cover; vol. 3 (1944) is illustrated with a scene from the motion picture on the cover.

Turkey. *Rüzgar Gibi Geçti* (Ankara: Baskent Yayinenvi, n.d.) 736 pp., casebound with jacket; a pirated edition.

Turkey. *Rüzgar Gibi Geçti* (Istanbul: Inzel Kitabevi, [1953?]) 426 pp., casebound with dust jacket; a pirated edition.

Turkey. *Rüzgar Gibi Geçti* (Istanbul: Ak Kitabevi, 1969) 1,022 pp., 2 vols., casebound with dust jackets; a pirated edition.

Turkey. *Rüzgar Gibi Geçti* (Istanbul: Altin Kitaplar Yayinevi, 1971) 664 pp., casebound with dust jacket; a pirated edition.

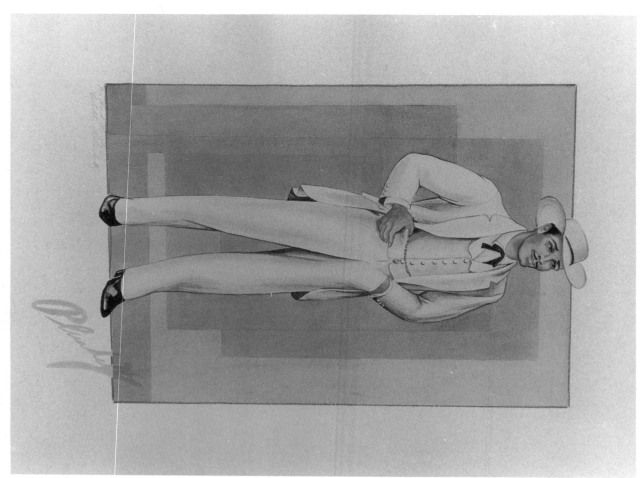

Rhett in a White Suit. A numbered print of a costume design by Walter Plunkett, reproduced by Jacob/Cortum Enterprises of Renondo Beach, California, in 1978 and signed by the artist. [16x20"]

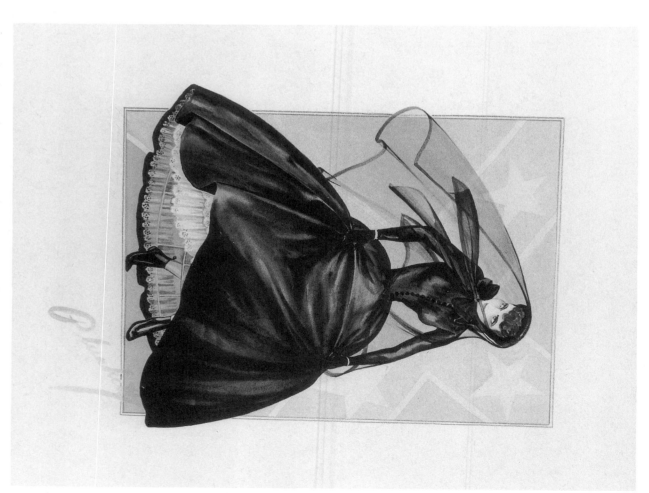

Scarlett in "Widow's Weeds". A numbered print of a costume design by Walter Plunkett, reproduced by Jacob/Cortum Enterprises of Renondo Beach, California, in 1978 and signed by the artist. [16x20"]

Advance Publicity and Promotion

Because Clark Gable was under contract to the Metro-Goldwyn-Mayer studios, David O. Selznick agreed to release *Gone with the Wind* through M-G-M in order to cast Gable in the role of Rhett Butler. As a result, all publicity and promotional material for the film was prepared and distributed by the advertising department of M-G-M rather than by Selznick and his company.

M-G-M produced a press book for *Gone with the Wind* as it did for every film it released in the U.S. and abroad. That book shows all of the advertising material available to local theaters for the promotion of *Gone with the Wind*. Among the many items produced for the promotion of *Gone with the Wind*, the colorful advertising posters designed for theater display are perhaps the most appealing to collectors.

"Campaign Book." This full-color cardboard folder contained the various sections of the *Gone with the Wind* Press Book. [17x19"]

When folded out, the inside cover of the campaign book revealed all of the available posters in full color. [27x41½"]

The back cover of the campaign book displayed the lobby cards available for use in theaters.

A detail view of the inside cover of the campaign book showing the three "24-sheet" posters available.

The original Press Book for *Gone with the Wind*
displays on its cover a photograph
of the Loew's Grand Theatre,
site of the world premiere
on 15 December 1939.
The Press Book is printed
on heavy enamel paper;
most of the 50 unnumbered
pages are cream in color.
[16x18"]

A detail view of the inside cover of the campaign book
showing available posters.

A page from the press book
displaying block posters and cards.

The back cover of the press book featured another
photograph of the Loew's Grand Theatre, and also displayed
the handmade lobby posters used inside the theater.

Following the premiere of *Gone with the Wind*, Eastman Kodak presented producer Selznick an award for "extraordinary achievement in the consumption of Eastman motion picture film." Whether the award celebrates the quantity of film Selznick's studio consumed or the quality of the final product is not entirely clear. The reverse of the cast aluminum trophy presented to Selznick is engraved with his photograph. [6½x6½"]

Selznick was also awarded the 1939 Photoplay Magazine Medal for *Gone with the Wind* as "The Best Photoplay of the Year." The medal, commissioned by Photoplay in 14 karat gold, was fashioned by Tiffany's in New York.

1939–1940 Theater Promotion

Preview Questionnaire: Members of the preview audience in Riverside, California, on 10 September 1939 were asked to complete this seven-item questionnaire and return it by mail to Selznick International Pictures.

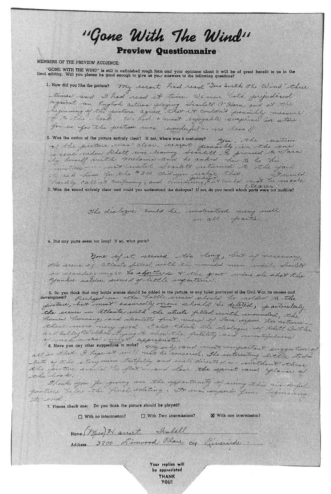

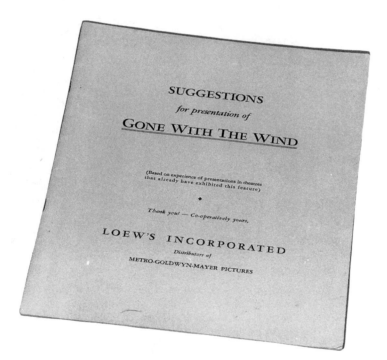

In this 12-page booklet, "Suggestions for Presentation of *Gone with the Wind*," David O. Selznick offered detailed instructions to theater managers for the presentation of his studio's film epic in 1940.

Theater "lobby cards" produced in 1939 include a card for the title credits and portraits of Clark Gable as Rhett Butler, Leslie Howard as Ashley Wilkes, Olivia de Havilland as Melanie Hamilton, Evelyn Keyes as Suellen O'Hara, Ann Rutherford as Careen O'Hara, Harry Davenport as Dr. Meade, Carroll Nye as Frank Kennedy, Laura Hope Crews as "Aunt Pittypat" Hamilton, Ona Munson as Belle Watling, Thomas Mitchell as Gerald O'Hara, Alicia Rhett as India Wilkes, Barbara O'Neil as Ellen O'Hara, and Hattie McDaniel as "Mammy." [11x14"]

The back cover of *The Washington Daily News* "Souvenir Edition" advertised "Romantic Fashions" based on designs from *Gone with the Wind* at $19.95.

The Washington Daily News published a 12-page "Souvenir Edition" on 26 January 1940 to celebrate *Gone with the Wind* with photos, articles, and advertisements.

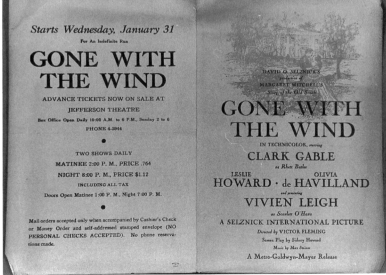

A program typical of those distributed free by theaters in 1940. [8x10"]

This full page advertisement for *Gone with the Wind* appeared in movie magazines early in 1940.

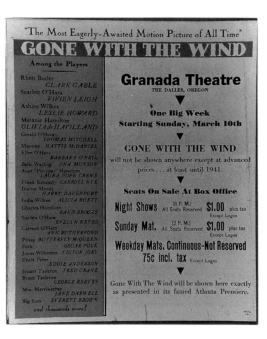

This particular example
of a herald advertises the engagement
of *Gone with the Wind* at the Granada Theatre
in The Dalles, Oregon, on 10-16 March 1940.

The front of a promotional herald
is illustrated with scenes from the film.
[8¼x10¼"]

"Scarlett Steps Out" in her burgundy party dress
on the cover of the graphic section of the *Chicago
Sunday Tribune* on 7 April 1940. An interview
with Vivien Leigh by Ed Sullivan
accompanied the color photograph.

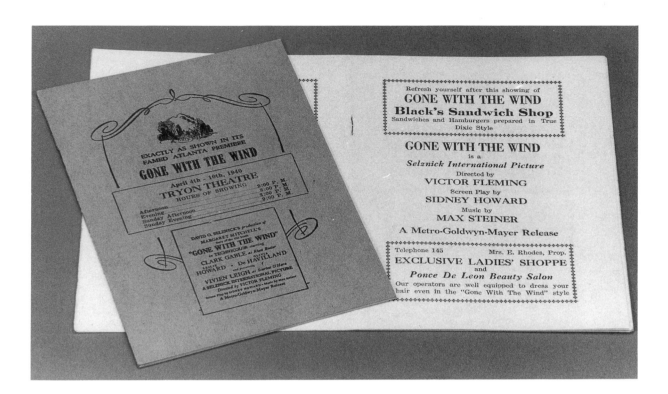

Some versions of the program distributed for *Gone with the Wind* allowed exhibitors to solicit advertising from local businesses. This 16-page example comes from the Tryon Theatre in Tryon, North Carolina, in April 1940. [5x7¼"]

Four tickets for the screening of *Gone with the Wind* at the Dillon Theatre in Dillon, South Carolina, on 13 April 1940.

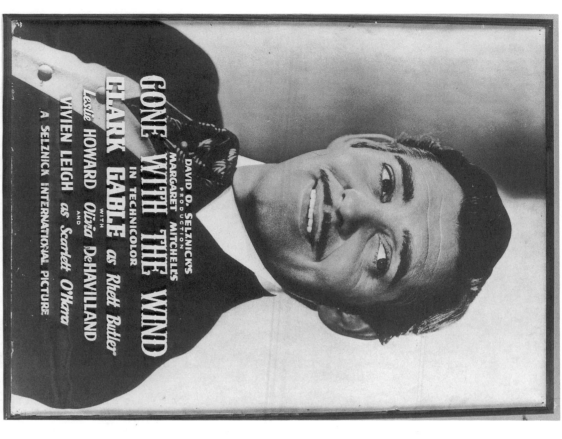

Clark Gable as Rhett Butler from an original poster board created by the poster artist of the Loew's Grand Theatre in Atlanta in 1940. [36x48"]

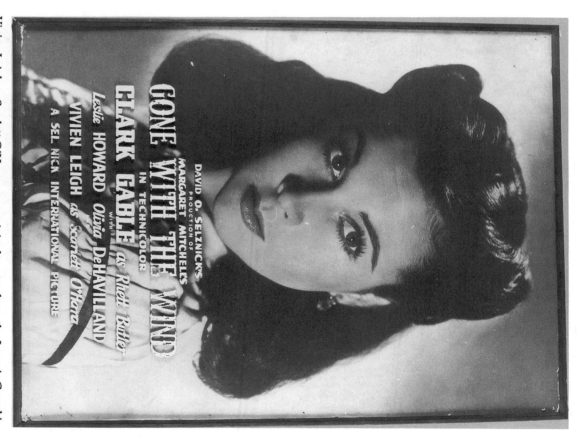

Vivien Leigh as Scarlett O'Hara on an original poster from the Loew's Grand in Atlanta. In those days Miss Leigh has not yet achieved equal billing with Mr. Gable, and her name was usually listed in the credits below those of Leslie Howard and Olivia de Havilland. [36x48"]

A desk blotter distributed by the Palace theatre in February 1942 promised that "You'll never BLOT this picture from your memory!" [4x9¼"]

Cartoonist Al Capp, whose comic strip "Lil' Abner" was approaching the peak of its popularity, satirized *Gone with the Wind* "Dogpatch Style" in the sequences beginning on Sunday, 4 October 1942.

A handmade poster board from the Loew's Grand in Atlanta, ca. 1942. The illustration originally mounted has been removed. [36x48½"]

Postwar Promotion

When the motion picture *Gone with the Wind* first appeared, war in Europe was already underway and the United States was thoroughly immersed in the struggle by the end of the film's first three-year run. Postwar audiences continued to clamor for *Gone with the Wind*, and M-G-M released the film for theater distribution every seven years—1947, 1954, 1961, and 1967–1968. In 1971, *Gone with the Wind* appeared in theaters again in combination with three other films on a "Fabulous Four" program.

1947

The 1947 Press Book, produced on newsprint in 16 pages, promoted *Gone with the Wind* as the picture "everybody wants to see." [11x15"]

Advertising posters appeared on the last page of the 1947 press book.

The 1947 lobby card bearing title credits is illustrated by a combination that would, in several versions, become perennial: Rhett with Scarlett in his arms against the background of Atlanta afire. [11x14"]

Lobby display materials
are offered on a page
of the 1947 press book.
[11x15"]

A "three-sheet" poster of 1947
stretched more than six feet in height.
[41x79"]

Another 1947 lobby card joined photo portraits of Gable and Leigh
in costume with two painted scenes from the film. [11x14"]

A large, "one-sheet" poster
from the 1947 release. [27x41"]

Although Miss Leigh's stardom
was well established by 1947,
this window card repeats her 1939 billing:
"And presenting Vivien Leigh as Scarlett O'Hara."

Rhett and Scarlett, caught up in a Confederate retreat, contemplate the lost glory of the South.

David O. Selznick's production "GONE WITH THE WIND"
in Technicolor

A Metro-Goldwyn-Mayer Release

Rhett and Scarlett dance together as the ladies of Atlanta hold a charity ball.

David O. Selznick's production "GONE WITH THE WIND"
in Technicolor

A Metro-Goldwyn-Mayer Release

Atlanta in flames—one of the most spectacular sights ever filmed.

David O. Selznick's production "GONE WITH THE WIND"
in Technicolor

A Metro-Goldwyn-Mayer Release

Hattie McDaniel as Mammy, Olivia DeHavilland as Melanie and Vivien Leigh as Scarlett view what remains of once-fabulous Tara Hall.

David O. Selznick's production "GONE WITH THE WIND"
in Technicolor

A Metro-Goldwyn-Mayer Release

Pictorial window cards left space at the top for the printing of information about the local theater and the dates when the film would be screened. [14x22"]

A very large 1961 poster displayed "12 Famous Scenes from 'Gone with the Wind'" with the query "How many do you remember?" [40x60"]

An insert poster for 1961. [14x36"]

Another poster from 1961 shares motifs in common with other promotional material for that year's release of the film. [27x41"]

Argentina. This 1940 poster for *Lo que el viento se llevo* shares art work with contemporary posters distributed in the United States; the title and credits appear in Spanish. [27x41"]

Australia. A large, one-sheet poster issued in 1968. [27x41"]

Belgium. A poster for *Autant en emporte le vent* printed in Brussels ca. 1947. [23x30½"]

Australia. This two-color, four-page theater program was distributed free by theaters in Sydney in 1940. Its cover notes that *Gone with the Wind* had been "approved by the censors as not suitable for general exhibition." [5¾x9"]

Brazil. This large poster for
E O Vento Levou employs
the artwork that has become
standard since 1968.
[29x41"]

Belgium. A similar poster
from the late 1940s. [23½x30"]

Belgium. A postcard of the 1950s repro-
duces the poster advertising *Autant
en emporte le vent*. [4x5¾"]

Canada. A 1954 lobby card from the United States has been altered
with a handwritten title for use in French-speaking
communities in Canada. [11x14"]

Denmark. A souvenir theater program for *Borte me Blæsten* distributed in the 1950s. [5½x7"]

Denmark. A four-page, two-color pamphlet promoted *Borte med Blæsten* ca. 1968. [9¾x13½"]

Chile. The cover of a theater program for *Lo que el viento se llevo* from the 1940s. [6x8½"]

Denmark. A poster from the 1960s. [24½x32"]

Finland. A poster distributed in 1950 advertises *Gone with the Wind* as *Tuulen Viemää* in Finnish and as *Borta med Vinden* in Swedish. [15¾x23"]

Chile. Inside the "programa" are a list of the cast, a summary of the plot, other credits, and a schedule of admission charges. [6x8½"]

Spain. A postcard-size promotional handout for *Lo que viento se llevo* used in the 1940s. [3x5"]

Spain. A souvenir photograph of Leslie Howard as Ashley Wilkes used as a publicity handout for *Lo que el viento se llevo* in 1951. [3x5"]

Spain/Spanish language. *Material de Propaganda*—lobby cards and posters—for *Lo que el viento se llevo* as displayed in the 1947 Spanish press book. [11x15"]

Spain/Spanish language. A large, one-sheet poster for *Lo que el viento se llevo* produced in the United States in 1947 for distribution in Spanish-speaking countries. [27x41"]

Spain/Spanish language. The MGM press book issued in 1947 for Spanish-speaking countries. [11x15"]

Spain. An advertising handbill for *Lo que el viento se llevo* distributed in Barcelona in March 1953. [5x7"]

Spain/Spanish language. A sample
of poster and advertising copy
for *Lo que el viento se llevo* is displayed
on a page of the 1954 Spanish
press book. [11x15½"]

Spain. A poster for *Lo que el viento se llevo*
printed in Barcelona in 1961. [22x39½"]

Spain. Samples of small advertising cards produced by
Infonal Rollfilm for *Lo que el viento se llevo* in the 1950s. [2½x4"]

Spain/Spanish language. A large poster produced in the United States in 1968 for distribution in Spanish-speaking countries promotes *Lo que el viento se llevo* in the 70mm format. [27x41"]

Spain/Spanish language. Another version of the poster for *Lo que el viento se llevo* circulated in 1968. [24½x32"]

Movie Life (February 1940) offered Rhett and Scarlett on its cover, backed by a fullpage advertisement for *Gone with the Wind* inside the cover.

Time (25 December 1939), diverted from its coverage of the war in Europe and the coming presidential election in the United States, devoted its Christmas cover to Scarlett O'Hara in her finery fashioned from the draperies of Tara. A review of the motion picture and a special report about Atlanta appeared inside.

The Family Circle (19 January 1940) gave rare prominence to Olivia de Havilland, costumed as Melanie Hamilton Wilkes, on its cover, but made her share it with cartoon characters and other exotic fauna.

Movies (February 1940) promised a story about its cover girl, Vivien Leigh, whose costume might well have given pause to even the irrepressible Scarlett O'Hara.

Hollywood (February 1940), with Rhett assisting a sullen Scarlett with her party dress on its cover, pondered a burning question: "Is Vivien Leigh a Real-Life Scarlett O'Hara?"

Silver Screen (February 1940), offering a stylized portrayal of the passionate lovers, proposed to tell its readers "How to Bring Out the Clark Gable in Any Man."

Click early in 1940 featured color and black and white photographs from *Gone with the Wind* in its report about the "Four Million Dollar Epic."

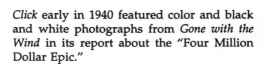

Woman's Own (11 May 1940) featured two pages of "Frocks from the World's Greatest Film" sketched by Peggy O'Neil.

Everywoman's (March 1940) visited Vivien Leigh at her home for a cover photo and article.

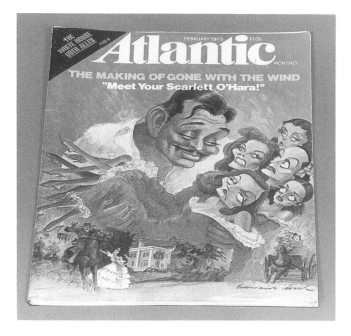

Modern Screen (June 1940) photographed Vivien Leigh for its cover in the same blouse that had appeared on the cover of *Everywoman's* in March. Her picture accompanied an article in which her fiancé Laurence Olivier was said to "insist" that he did not wish to be called "a great lover."

Atlantic (February 1973) commissioned a parody of the most often used advertising motif for *Gone with the Wind* to promote the first of two articles by Gavin Lambert about "The Making of Gone with the Wind"; the second of the articles appeared in its March issue.

Motion Picture (February 1941) presented Rhett comforting Scarlett on its cover with a story about the success of *Gone with the Wind*.

Quick (7 May 1951) offered a 12-year-old photograph of Vivien Leigh costumed as Scarlett for Ashley's birthday party to accompany its article about "Hollywood's New Matinee Idols."

TV Guide (6-12 November 1976) promoted the television premiere of *Gone with the Wind* with a cover story about "The Battles Behind the Making of the Movie."

161

Madame Alexander used a picture of Vivien Leigh—not one of its dolls!—in its national advertising in 1939 and 1940.

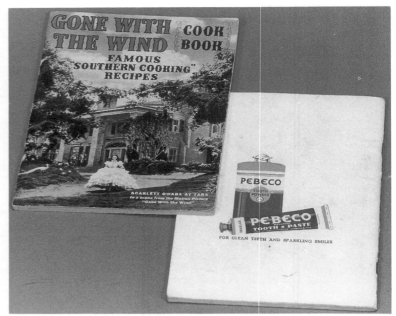

This *Gone with the Wind Cook Book* was given away with the purchase of a large tube of PEBECO toothpaste. The 48-page, paperbound book contained 125 "Southern" recipes and was copyrighted in 1940 by Lehn and Fink Products.

"Scarlett O'Hara" by Madame Alexander led the list of new dolls in the Sears, Roebuck catalogue in 1940, at an advertised price of $2.79.

A magazine advertisement offering the *Gone with the Wind Cook Book* with the purchase of PEBECO toothpaste.

Scarlett and Rhett are both represented on the front and back covers of a *Gone with the Wind* paper doll book produced in Chicago by Merrill Publishing in 1940.

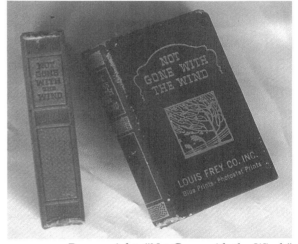

Paperweight: "*Not* Gone with the Wind." Promotional for Louis Frey Co., Inc., ca. 1940.

A series of small, boxed "Scarlett O'Hara" games was manufactured and sold by Marietta Games of Marietta, Ohio, in 1940. Pictured here are "Scarlett O'Hara: Hour Glass," "Scarlett O'Hara: One of Her Problems," and "Scarlett O'Hara: ?" Each game is supplied with board and small marbles and is played under rules similar to Chinese checkers.

Gone with the Wind neckties for men, made of polyester by Britannia ca. 1976, featured scenes from the motion picture and were sold for $7.50 each.

[left] A linen kitchen calendar, produced in Romania for Franco Manufacturing of New York, celebrated *Gone with the Wind* in 1977. [18 x 29]

[right] This envelope packaged the 1977 linen kitchen calendar.

[below] "Scarlett" is the first of a series of *Gone with the Wind* collector plates produced by Edwin M. Knowles China Company in 1978. [8½" diameter]

[below, left] "Mammy Lacing Scarlett" is the fifth of the Knowles China Company series of collector plates. [8½ diameter]

Seeds for Scarlett O'Hara Morning Glories were marketed for 39¢ a package in 1978 and 49 cents in 1980 by Northrup King Seeds of Minneapolis.

This leaflet promoted the "very special" *Gone with the Wind* Gray Line bus tour operated in Atlanta during the 1970s.

A *Gone with the Wind* Pilgrimage was one of the sightseeing excursions packaged by Gray Line Tours in Atlanta during the 1970s.

Fujaira (United Arab Emirates) issued postage stamps bearing portraits of Vivien Leigh and Clark Gable and photographs of scenes from *Gone with the Wind* during the 1970s.

A figurine of Rhett and Scarlett, about 10" tall, was manufactured in Japan in a limited edition of 2,500.

"Rhett" and "Scarlett" dolls were produced by Peggy Nesbitt Doll Company in England during the 1970s.

Individual porcelain figures of Scarlett and Rhett, 5¾" tall, were marketed by Avon Products in 1983.